INTRODUCTION

Beginnings are important.

Many of the great first lines in literature echo through the ages because they set the tone for everything that is to follow. From Charles Dickens's "It was the best of times, it was the worst of times," to Jane Austen's "It is a truth universally acknowledged, that a single man in possession of a good fortune, must be in want of a wife," the start of the story can sweep us off our feet and propel us into a fantastical future before we are even fully aware of what's happening.

It makes sense then, that as Christians, we should pay attention to how the stories of the gospels start; they set the tone for everything that is to follow. From Matthew's "An account of the genealogy of Jesus the Messiah, the son of David, the son of Abraham" to John's "In the beginning was the Word, and the Word was with God, and the Word was God," each of the four gospel writers offers a unique perspective on who Jesus is and how he changes our lives. Each gospel begins the narrative in a distinct way that helps us encounter Jesus anew. From Matthew's careful lineage to Mark's sense of urgency to Luke's majestic *Magnificat* to John's cosmic scope, we can learn something fresh about Jesus and about ourselves by paying attention to how the start of each story sets the tone for our life of faith.

This Advent, we invite you to "start at the very beginning; it's a very good place to start." This daily devotional spends a week with each of the four gospels, exploring how the writers tell the story of Jesus through their unique perspectives. The authors of *Gospel Voices* walk us through the gospel writer's themes, how they start the story, favorite passages, and examples of how to live out the gospel. The devotions include collects from the Book of Common Prayer to help frame each section and a weekly opportunity for *Lectio Divina,* an ancient way of praying through scripture. You can read each day's devotional on your own or as part of a small group study to help strengthen your faith in this holy season. And, of course, on various years, Christmas falls on different days in the fourth week of Advent, so we've included the full week and invite you to read through it as well.

Beginnings are important. And part of the great good news of God is that every year in Advent, each of us gets the gift of a new beginning, a fresh start. Whether you have done daily devotionals for years or this is your first one, whether you've read the Bible from cover to cover or you are opening a Bible for the first time, whether you are an expert in prayer or you are just starting out, this book, and this season, is for you.

I wonder what you will hear when you listen to the story this time?

I wonder how you will start the story of Jesus that you tell others?

Are you ready? Let's begin.

The Rev. Melody Wilson Shobe
Chief of Staff, Forward Movement

GOSPEL VOICES

Advent with Matthew, Mark, Luke, & John

TINA FRANCIS, JERUSALEM JACKSON GREER,
DEON K. JOHNSON, & MARSHALL JOLLY

Forward Movement
Cincinnati, Ohio

#2706

978-0-88028-532-2

THE FIRST WEEK OF ADVENT

MATTHEW

Hope in the Fulfillment of God's Covenant

This Week's Writer
TINA FRANCIS

SUNDAY

I do not know what brought you to this text today. Maybe you're procrastinating on a deadline. Maybe this is a last-ditch attempt to salvage a difficult year. Maybe you're desperate enough to stop scrolling and let the room get quiet for a second. All of these are ways of arriving. None of them disqualifies you. All of that is welcome.

Advent often comes when people are already full. Full of worry, of unfinished conversations, of days that do not quite add up. It is called a season of waiting, but not because waiting is virtuous. Sometimes waiting is all that's left. Advent does not bring easy answers in a tiny, color-coded folder. It plops down beside us, out of breath, and says, *Yes. This is heavy.*

The Gospel of Matthew was written for people living in that kind of moment. Matthew is a teacher trying to help a community that is grieving what has been lost and is uncertain about what remains. The world they trusted has shattered. Matthew knows this ground well. Jesus is gone. The disciples have scattered. Rome is more Rome-ish than usual. Everyone is asking the same urgent question: *What now? How do we live now?*

Matthew answers in an unexpected way. He begins with a genealogy... a list of names. Generally, that is the least compelling way to begin anything. But Matthew is saying that before we talk about Jesus, we must talk about where he comes from. History matters. What shaped us and bruised us matters. Before we talk about God-with-us, we need to name who "us" actually is.

"Us" turns out to be complicated, full of scoundrels and saints. And Matthew leaves the mess in. The ones who did real damage and didn't get redacted. Complicated people. Generations marked by failure, violence, and grief. Matthew insists that God works through actual lives, not ideal ones. That is either deeply comforting or deeply inconvenient, once you realize that it includes you.

This conviction runs through everything Matthew writes. Strip away the church words, and you can hear questions that sound suspiciously familiar:

How do I honor my roots without being trapped by them?

How do I live rightly without becoming brittle or cruel?

How do we recognize God's presence not later, not elsewhere, but here?

What does it cost to follow Jesus when the price is felt in the body, in relationships, in ordinary decisions?

Matthew doesn't answer these questions with pithy catchphrases or spiritual platitudes. He gives us Jesus teaching. Sermons. Parables. Instructions meant to be tried, not admired. How to forgive without disappearing. How to handle money without letting it hollow you out. How to pray when words feel thin or dishonest.

Jesus teaches us how to live together when power is uneven, fear is loud, and love is misunderstood. That is to say, Jesus teaches us how to live most days of the week.

In Matthew, preparation for Christ is not about being spiritually shiny. It is about formation. Small, ordinary choices made again and again until mercy feels like muscle memory. Like instinct. Love that shows up quietly, without a press release. Habits, not heroics.

Discipleship is not a vibe. It is work. Awkward, inconvenient work. Here is the part nobody puts on a mug: faithfulness is inefficient. It interrupts you. It will wreck your schedule. It will ask you to choose love over convenience, again and again.

Matthew does not promise this will fix what is broken. What he gives us instead is something sturdy to hold onto. Emmanuel. God with us. With us in the half-baked, half-brave, half-built parts of our story. With us when progress is slow. With us when we take five steps backward for every two steps forward.

Maybe that is the invitation today. Not to feel ready. Just to notice. To choose one small, inconvenient act of faithfulness. And to stay.

Almighty God, give us grace to cast away the works of darkness, and put on the armor of light, now in the time of this mortal life in which your Son Jesus Christ came to visit us in great humility; that in the last day, when he shall come again in his glorious majesty to judge both the living and the dead, we may rise to the life immortal; through him who lives and reigns with you and the Holy Spirit, one God, now and for ever. Amen.

MONDAY

Matthew begins the way old women begin stories when the night is long and the lamps burn low: with a roll call of names. Names that start to click against one another like prayer beads sliding through a practiced hand. Matthew is not a man who hurries the holy. He takes his time, bead to bead, name to name, until what sounds ordinary begins to hum with something more. At first glance, the opening of Matthew's Gospel reads like the ancient world's phone book—a dry, bureaucratic list. Names blur. Begats pile up. The instinct is to skip ahead to angels and dreams and a baby. But Matthew insists we slow down. He starts here on purpose.

This list is not filler. It is defiant. It is a quiet refusal to erase the people whose blood and bone made room for the Messiah. Matthew knows whose names are usually left out. This is not a sanitized bloodline. It is a real one, with complicated histories, their pasts rattling behind them.

This family tree is crooked. It leans. It has knots. It has branches snapped by storms and grafted back on. Kings who abused power. Men who failed spectacularly. Women who survived impossible situations with grit and holy defiance. Tamar. Rahab. Bathsheba. People whose stories are not neat, not polite, not easy to explain at dinner.

Matthew could have pruned the family tree for polite company. He does not. He leaves the mess in the story because the mess is how God comes—through real families. Through the fault lines of human history. Through stories that carry shame and possibility at the same time.

Jesus arrives bearing the weight of what came before him. Not protected from it. Not hovering above it. Fully entangled.

What does this tell us about Jesus? It tells us that he does not drop into history untouched. He does not arrive sealed off from grief or harm. He comes carrying it. All of it. The weight of what came before. The ache. The longing. The courage. The damage. He enters history fully, not to erase it, but to redeem it from the inside.

The genealogy is not a highlight reel. It is a family album—the kind with pages you might want to tear out and throw away. But Matthew says: *Keep them.* All of them. God doesn't need perfection. God works with *what is.*

Jesus is shaped by women who had to make impossible choices. By outsiders who survived by their wits. By men who made terrible decisions and still became part of the story. He comes from people who were faithful sometimes and reckless at others. Brave and broken in the same breath.

Jesus is not God's escape plan from humanity. He is God's commitment to it.

That means your story is not in the way. Your family. Your history. The parts you wish were different. These are not obstacles. They are where God starts.

Jesus comes from imperfect people.

That is the point.

REFLECT

Think about your family tree. Who are the people you'd rather not claim? How do their stories—and the stories of all the people in your family history—shape you? What is the Gospel of Matthew saying to us through the purposeful beginning of a litany of genealogy?

TUESDAY

The prayer practice of *Lectio Divina* is a simple Christian practice with a fancy Latin name. The idea is straightforward: you read a short passage from scripture, notice the word or phrase that won't stop tapping you on the shoulder, and you don't swat it away. You stay with it.

This practice began centuries ago in monasteries, back when people prayed with scripture the way you listen to a song on repeat, catching a new phrase each time.

That's *lectio*. You read. You linger. You pray. You marinate. You let the words get a little bossy.

Over time, it starts to say something back. Not in a booming-voice-from-the-sky way, but more in an

I think my houseplant is trying to tell me something way. It slows you down long enough for God to get a word in—often about something you didn't know you needed.

For this practice, I chose a scripture I know almost too well: the Lord's Prayer found in Matthew 6:9-13. I read it straight through, then slowed down, like easing a car off the highway, waiting to see what would emerge.

The word that rose was daily: *Give us this day our daily bread.*

There's something almost disappointing about the word daily. I wanted something sharper—temptation, trespass, deliverance—something with teeth. Yet daily is what came. Plain as toast.

Daily resists my instinct to stockpile reassurance or outrun tomorrow. It insists on return. On asking again, on trust practiced more than once. It leaves no room to pretend I won't need help again tomorrow. I want a God who hands me guarantees, but this prayer hands me a day.

The Greek word here is *epiousion*, a strange word that appears almost nowhere else. Its meaning hovers between what is needed now and what is needed to keep us going—bread for this day, and the day coming toward us.

Epiousion does not promise abundance. It promises continuity. Bread that keeps a body alive and a story moving. Bread that spoils when hoarded. Bread that teaches the mouth how to ask again.

Daily bread assumes hunger. Real hunger. Work that must be done again tomorrow. It assumes we are not self-sufficient, no matter how convincing our calendars and contingency plans appear.

I notice how much energy I spend trying to escape the daily. I want resolution, not repetition. Assurance, not dependence. A plan that stretches further than today. But this prayer keeps returning me to enough. Enough for this day. Enough to stay present. Enough to trust that tomorrow will ask its own questions.

Epiousion lives where Advent lives—between now and not yet. Waiting here is not empty. It is attentive. Hope sounds less like certainty and more like asking for bread and believing it will come.

Bread for today.
Bread for the coming day.
Bread necessary for being alive at all.

Give us this day our daily bread. Not just me, but us—our shared need.

If you want to try *Lectio Divina*, read the Lord's Prayer once, slowly. Notice the word that tugs at you. Sit with it. See where it follows you.

Today's word for me was daily. Tomorrow, it may be something else. That, too, is part of the prayer.

PRACTICE

Using the practice of *Lectio Divina*, spend time with this passage from Matthew. To prepare your mind and heart, start with a moment of silence. Then read the passage slowly, perhaps two or three times. Think about a word or phrase that captures your attention. Then meditate on that word, asking why it resonates in this moment. Respond to God in prayer, and then rest in silence, savoring the word and contemplating what God is saying to you. Finally, consider how this word or phrase is calling you to act.

> Matthew 6:9-13: *Our Father in heaven, hallowed be your name. Your kingdom come. Your will be done, on earth as it is in heaven. Give us this day our daily bread. And forgive us our debts, as we also have forgiven our debtors. And do not bring us to the time of trial, but rescue us from the evil one.*

WEDNESDAY

Joseph did not set out to raise the Son of God. He was a carpenter, which is to say he knew something about pressure and patience. He knew that wood had limits. Push too hard, and it splits. He knew to measure twice, to wait for the grain to tell you which way it wants to go. He wanted a simple life. A wife. A job. Some children.

And then Mary tells him she is pregnant.

Scripture says, with heroic understatement, that "Joseph considered this." I picture him awake in the middle of the night with the ceiling fan of his mind whirring. Sitting on the edge of a low wooden bed. Elbows on knees. Hands in his hair. Outside, a donkey complains about something, as donkeys do, which does not help. Inside, the math does not work.

Nothing about this moment feels holy. It feels unforgiving and dangerous.

And this—this tentative, unsafe, middle place—is where the story of Jesus begins. Just a young man sitting with a choice that feels heavier the longer he holds it. Joseph understands the stakes even if he doesn't have language for them. He knows what happens to women whose stories don't line up. He knows that the law gives him a clean exit and that, in this moment, it would come at her expense.

Scripture says Joseph is righteous—*dikaios*, which we often hear as rule-keeping. But Joseph's righteousness looks like hesitation. Like restraint. Like a carpenter who knows that force, applied too quickly, causes damage that can't be undone. Like deciding that someone else's life matters more than his own reputation. Joseph's obedience is protective. Someone vulnerable is depending on him to choose mercy.

Clarity comes later, if it comes at all. Joseph acts first. He chooses Mary without knowing whether this will end in safety or simply more trouble. There is no small parade waiting at the end of the road for doing the merciful thing.

The family that forms around this child is complicated from the start. Marked by scandal. Shaped by fear.

Forced to move when staying would be dangerous. They depend on the kindness of strangers. On doors that open just enough. On hands that pass bread without asking too many questions. They learn how to live small enough to survive. Jesus grows up inside a story full of displacement and unfairness and decisions made under pressure.

Matthew calls the child Emmanuel, which sounds lovely until you remember its origin. Isaiah spoke it during invasion and panic and political chaos. Emmanuel, God is with you, not later, not once things calm down, but while the danger is so close you can hear it breathing.

That's Advent hope: not rescue, but presence that stays put.

Joseph eventually fades out of the story. We know he stayed long enough to teach the boy how to use his hands. How to wait. How to notice when pressure will snap what you're trying to build. Then he is gone, having done what faithful people so often do: he made room. He chose mercy and left no record of it.

Perhaps this is obedience—the risky, ordinary work of protecting life while the world is unsteady and choosing to stay anyway. Maybe obedience has less to do with certainty than with attention, with the small, stubborn practice of staying awake to what God asks when the night offers no explanations. Joseph does not tame the fear. He says yes to the risk. He lets his yes move into his body, into the grain of his days, into the future he thought he knew by heart.

And what if obedience is not heroic at all, but intimate? The kind that shows up on roads you never planned to take. The kind that keeps company with what is fragile. Joseph consents to the risk, not because it feels good or noble, but because love is already there, asking to be protected.

Obedience, then, does not promise safety. It opens you to the wild, inconvenient nearness of God. You carry what you can. You leave what you must. You learn, slowly, how to stay. And in that staying, something like joy takes root, not because the world is steady, but because love is.

REFLECT

Ponder the story of Joseph. Imagine yourself in his position. How would you respond to the news? What does it mean to choose mercy without fanfare, to be obedient without desiring a hero's welcome? How can Joseph's example inspire you to live faithfully?

O God, who from the family of your servant David did raise up Joseph to be the guardian of your incarnate Son and the spouse of his virgin mother: Give us grace to imitate his uprightness of life and his obedience to your commands; through the same your Son Jesus Christ our Lord, who lives and reigns with you and the Holy Spirit, one God, for ever and ever. Amen.

THURSDAY

My favorite story in Matthew's Gospel is the faceoff between Jesus and the Syrophoenician woman. Let's be honest, though: this is not exactly the first choice when we think of heartwarming Advent stories.

We prefer more straightforward stories. Take the Prodigal Son. There's drama, intrigue, a bad decision spiral, followed by regret, reconciliation, and an emotional reunion that ends with a party. A single tear rolls down our cheek. We exhale happily. What's not to love?

The encounter between Jesus and the Syrophoenician woman found in Matthew 15:21-28 is not even in the same zip code. It resists easy answers. And that's why I love it.

A little context helps. Matthew tells us Jesus is in the region of Tyre and Sidon, foreign and unfamiliar territory. When the Gospel of Mark recounts this story, we learn that Jesus doesn't want anyone to know he's holed up in a house. Maybe he needed a nap after a brutal travel day. Maybe he was just being prudent and trying to stay safe. Or maybe Jesus had simply used up all his words for the day. Either way, it's clear that he's keeping a low profile.

But this unnamed Canaanite (Syrophoenician) woman, our beloved protagonist, has crossed many borders—geographical, cultural, and religious. She arrives empty-handed and loud with need.

She shouts to Jesus, "Have mercy on me... my daughter is tormented."

Jesus explains that he was sent only to the lost in "the house of Israel."

She drops to her knees and says, "Lord, help me."

For centuries, people have clutched their pearls at this next part. Jesus says, "It is not fair to take the children's food and throw it to the dogs."

You could cut the tension with a Santoku knife.

Calm. Clear. Undeterred. She retorts, "Even the dogs eat the crumbs that fall from their masters' table."

She does not deny the system. She exposes it. She insists mercy is available. Matthew does not tell us what Jesus feels. He tells us what happens.

"Woman," Jesus says, "great is your faith! Let it be done," and her daughter is instantly healed.

I don't claim to understand all the elements of this story; I only know that this prophetic woman widened mercy. Her story doesn't sentimentalize faith. This is what faith looks like stripped of manners. When the stakes are high and love is on the line, faith may sound disruptive, look abrasive, and feel deeply vulnerable.

We do ourselves a disservice when we equate passive waiting with virtue. But this resourceful mother did not confuse obedience with holiness. She "waits" by showing up. She believes God is reachable, that even resistance is just part of the sacred conversation.

I know this woman. I've been her. I've prayed shameless, uncensored prayers. I've begged for outcomes that are embarrassing to admit. I've dropped to my knees in prayer in hallways, bathrooms, and kitchen floors. I know the frenetic determination that takes over a mother when her child is suffering.

This story shows us what Advent really asks of us. Waiting is not quiet or polite. It is the courage to risk failure. To risk rejection. To risk humiliation. Hope, here, is not a fleeting feeling, but a muscle worked. It is labor. And it is love.

The door may not open right away. But the knock endures.

STUDY

Read Matthew 15:21-28:

> *Jesus left that place and went away to the district of Tyre and Sidon. Just then a Canaanite woman from that region came out and started shouting, "Have mercy on me, Lord, Son of David; my daughter is tormented by a demon." But he did not answer her at all. And his disciples came and urged him, saying, "Send her away, for she keeps shouting after us." He answered, "I was sent only to the lost sheep of the house of Israel." But she came and knelt before him, saying, "Lord, help me." He answered, "It is not fair to take the children's food and throw it to the dogs." She said, "Yes, Lord, yet even the dogs eat the crumbs that fall from their masters' table." Then Jesus answered her, "Woman, great is your faith! Let it be done for you as you wish." And her daughter was healed instantly.*

The woman defies social norms for the sake of her daughter. What is something you care about deeply enough to pursue with boldness? Have there been times when you confused holiness with politeness? What would a more honest, uncensored prayer life look like?

FRIDAY

I was profoundly lost in my twenties.

Not in a dramatic way. More like a slow ache. I did everything I was supposed to do and still felt unmoored. The financial crisis of 2008 was unfolding, and like so many others, I struggled to find work. I worked hard at many jobs, from a call center to hosting tables, nowhere near my education or my strengths.

I was living with my parents—because Indian families do that. Truthfully, we needed each other. My parents had sacrificed so much when they immigrated to North America for their children, and I wanted desperately to honor that. I longed to be useful, called, and anchored. Instead, I was sinking into a kind of existential quicksand.

What made the waiting unbearable was hunger. Hunger for meaning. For belonging. For some assurance that my life was moving somewhere hopeful. Still, I showed up for my family, my church, my responsibilities, while quietly wondering if my purpose and vocation had passed me by.

Then I received an invitation.

An Anglican priest in South Africa invited me to join a small, global circle of women for a theology intensive in Burundi. I told her she had the wrong person. I knew nothing about theology.

"Trust me," she smiled knowingly.

I said yes. I worked, saved, boarded planes, and arrived at Lake Tanganyika to meet ten women, soon to be kin, from South Africa to Colombia.

Our guiding text was *Doing Theology with an Eye on Mary*. Its premise was enchanting: Mary was already a theologian, long before there was even a word for it. Her womb was a site of theology, where divinity took flesh.

Mary's waiting unfolds in a triad pattern.

First, she is blessed: "You who are highly favored," proclaims the angel. Before comprehension, there is belovedness. Her identity precedes calling. Hope sparks when worth is named—often before it is felt.

Then comes trust: embodied and costly. Mary's yes is not abstract. She opens her body to a future she cannot secure or explain. Waiting becomes a daily act of courage, growing the unseen.

Finally, there is communion. Mary goes to Elizabeth because waiting alone is unbearable. Hope needs witnesses. Two women sharing stories, symptoms, and solidarity. Hope, I learned, is a muscle strengthened in community.

It's wonderful that the Gospel of Matthew as a whole mirrors a similar pattern for waiting. Jesus begins with blessing. Not advice or admonition. Blessing. "Blessed are..." he says, speaking dignity into people long denied it. Then he asks for trust that is small and embodied, like a mustard seed. Over and over, hope is sustained not through ideas but through care: meals shared, bodies healed, the overlooked brought back into view. The soul, it turns out, does not survive on certainty. It survives on being seen.

As I reflect on my life, I can see this trifold pattern: blessing came first, an unmerited invitation. Then a small, bodily act of trust. I said yes. Then care, given and received, in a circle of women.

Fifteen years ago, I did not know that this trip—this small, trembling yes—would become a holy marker on the long road guiding me toward the priesthood.

I only knew that something had shifted, and that hope had returned quietly, enough to keep me moving.

The question, dear pilgrim, is not how we survive the waiting. It is how we practice hope while we wait.

CONSIDER

Where do you need to be named and blessed again?

What small act of trust is already within reach?

Who could you accompany, so that their waiting becomes, at least for a time, more bearable?

SATURDAY

"My umbilical cord is buried here."

She says this without ceremony. We are standing on the grounds of St. Michael's Episcopal Church in Farmington, New Mexico. In Diné tradition, the baby's umbilical cord is buried on family land, so they always have a place to return. The land is given custody. Before a child speaks, before a single choice is made, the earth has already learned their name. *You belong*, the land whispers.

Her parents buried her umbilical cord on church grounds. "They prayed I would return," she laughs. "And I did!"

Rev. Cornelia is a priest. A poet. A storyteller. A fly fisher. A caretaker of sheep. She speaks of land with the same gravitas she brings to scripture. Her faith is shaped by

Hózhó, a way of living that insists on harmony, beauty, and right relationship.

"Sheep are sacred for us," she says as we walk through her family's sheep camp. "They are our relatives." Diné women have a special connection with sheep. In their hands, wool becomes rugs, blankets, clothing—chaos pulled into pattern by hand and memory.

Cornelia is spending the day with us, a motley crew of sunburnt adults and sweaty children visiting from St. Julian of Norwich in Austin, Texas. For twelve summers now, we have caravanned to Farmington. We call it a pilgrimage, which sounds impressive. But what brings us back is something simpler: friendship.

When I think of a faith community that truly lives out the gospel, Cornelia and her community come to mind. The Diné were forcibly removed from their land. Cornelia knows what it means for a people to have their dignity assaulted: children forced into schools, names replaced, language punished, hair cut. Her generosity is not naïve or sentimental. It is a choice. A costly one.

For the Diné, hair is an extension of their life force, a living connection to ancestors, where prayer and memory are held. To cut it by force was spiritual violence. A deep rupture. A public unmaking.

This is where the gospel becomes visible. In the Beatitudes, Jesus speaks directly to those who have lost land, body, and name. "Blessed are those who mourn. Blessed are those who hunger." Jesus does not promise escape. He promises inheritance—not through seizing, burning, or extracting, but through staying. "They will inherit the earth."

Inheritance, here, is embodied. It is communal. It begins before a child can speak.

When the child is still in the womb, the community gathers to bless the mother into strength. Elders burn sacred herbs. Cornmeal is rubbed on the body. Songs rise through breath and muscle. Men tend the ceremonial fire. Women bake *Alkaan*, a blue cornmeal cake, cooked slowly in the ground, stones heated, batter laid down, earth drawn back over it. This is not culinary duty but devotion. *Alkaan* becomes a shared meal, communion with land and ancestors.

This ceremony was for Cornelia's daughter, and for her granddaughter, only 13 days earthside. Her "little granny girl," already stitched into the earth's remembering.

Cornelia led us to the spot where her daughter's placenta was buried. She closed her eyes, lifted her face to the sun, and smiled. Was it prayer or memory? I will never know. Whatever it was, it felt like standing in right relationship with creation. The ground had been trusted with life. I felt the weight of that trust and knew we were standing on holy ground.

The land archives whatever love entrusts to it—umbilical cords, placentas, prayers. Maybe mercy works the same way.

May it be so.

ACT

Small mercies don't announce themselves. They wait longer than is efficient. Listen without correcting. Bring food and do not ask for the story. Learn how to say someone's name correctly. Bonus: spell it out phonetically in your Notes App for next time.

Return—to the same person, the same place—when it would be easy to disappear. Small mercies are offered rides, rolling out a single parent's garbage bin to the curb on garbage day, and remembering dates, good or bad. Apologize without explanation. Speak gently to a tired body—yours or another's.

Stay.

MARK

The Voice in the Wilderness

This Week's Writer
MARSHALL JOLLY

SUNDAY

What are we to make of the person—the saint—whom tradition more than history has dubbed Mark? More importantly, how does the gospel that bears his name call us to prepare for the coming of Christ?

Mark's Gospel has always appeared second after Matthew; it is the shortest of the four, contains no birth, infancy, or adolescent narratives of Jesus, and forgoes any genealogy. It begins with Jesus's baptism and ends not with the high point of the resurrection but with the women leaving an empty tomb, too afraid to tell anyone. So dissatisfying was the gospel's ending that early Christians offered not one but two alternative endings, which survive in the canon today.

Much less is known about the person who wrote the gospel. Luke tells us in Acts that Mark was an associate of Peter and Paul, and Paul reveals in Colossians that Mark and Barnabas were cousins. Mark may have served as Peter's secretary, and several traditions suggest that Mark's Gospel was composed with heavy reliance on his ministry alongside Peter. Tradition holds that Mark traveled to Alexandria and founded the church there, served as its first bishop, and was martyred in 68 CE.

The second-century bishop Irenaeus, drawing on the imagery of the "four living creatures" in Ezekiel and Revelation, assigned each of the four gospels an iconographic symbol. He gave the Gospel of Mark the symbol of the lion—a reference to the prophecy in Isaiah 40, fulfilled by John the Baptist in the first sentences of the gospel.

From the beginning, Mark's Gospel moves at a brisk pace. Things do not just happen, they happen immediately—a word that appears more than forty times in this gospel; more than everywhere else in the New Testament, combined.

As we listen closely to the Gospel of Mark's voice this week, let us attend to the word "immediately." How might our preparations to receive Christ be shaped and challenged by a sense of what is immediate? Are the things immediately before us the things that God desires for us? What might it mean for us to wait and watch and wonder with a renewed sense of the immediacy Mark's Gospel conveys?

The voice of the Prophet rings forth as a lion with an urgent—an immediate—word for us: "The kingdom of God has come near; repent, and believe in the good news."

Merciful God, who sent your messengers the prophets to preach repentance and prepare the way for our salvation: Give us grace to heed their warnings and forsake our sins, that we may greet with joy the coming of Jesus Christ our Redeemer; who lives and reigns with you and the Holy Spirit, one God, now and for ever. Amen.

MONDAY

The first person we meet in Mark's Gospel is not Jesus or Mary or Joseph or an angel; it's John the Baptizer. Mark gives us quite the introduction! "Now John was clothed with camel's hair, with a leather belt around his waist, and he ate locusts and wild honey" (Mark 1:6). Though this description might befuddle the modern ear, it would have met the ancient ear with notes of familiarity, echoing the description of Elijah in 2 Kings or Zechariah's depiction of prophets in general.

Generally speaking, the job of the biblical prophet is not all that desirable by modern standards. Jeremiah was flogged and thrown down a well, Hosea was commanded by God to marry an unfaithful spouse, Isaiah is said to have been sawn in two, and even John the Baptizer would soon have his own head parted from him. The schoolchildren weren't exactly raising their hands to tell their teachers they might want to be prophets when they grow up!

Nevertheless, prophets are a hallmark of Judeo-Christian history and identity. A prophet is not simply someone who says hard things that people need to hear. By that metric, any therapist or preacher worth their salt would meet the mark. Rather, prophets not only challenge how things are but also realign the heart so that what we've come to expect can make room for the unexpected movements of God in our midst. This is certainly true of John the Baptizer.

Other gospel writers give us details about John the Baptizer's parentage or fuller accounts of his teaching, but Mark, in his direct and unadorned way, comes straight to the point: John is sent ahead of Jesus to prepare the way, as one crying out in the wilderness, just as Isaiah had prophesied. (The careful reader will note that while Mark 1:3 is a quotation of Isaiah 40:3, Mark 1:2b does not appear in Isaiah and is likely a conflation of verses from Malachi and Exodus.)

Mark is also clear that John is up to something: baptizing as an act of repentance so that sins can be forgiven. Even busy folks from the metropolis of Jerusalem were going into the country to hear John preach in Judea and receive his baptism—a reversal of the usual flow from country to city of people and commerce. What was it about John's message that caused people to set aside what they had come to expect—their everyday lives, the city they had come to know, the rhythm of work and rest—and journey into the embodiment of the unexpected, the wilderness? What longing of the human heart or soul would necessitate such a journey?

REFLECT

As we pray and ponder over John the Baptizer's unusual attire and unexpected message, let us also consider where we hear the voice of the prophets in our own day. Who are they? What message do they have to deliver to us? Where in our lives do we need to leave the status quo and risk journeying into the wilderness of the unexpected and unknown?

TUESDAY

Lectio Divina is not an academic endeavor—we do not seek to interpret or exegete the chosen passage. Rather, as with prayer itself, we begin with inviting God to come among us and to reveal Godself to us through this holy text. The practice has four parts or "moves": reading (*lectio*), meditating (*meditatio*), speaking (*oratio*), and contemplating (*contemplatio*).

Let us utilize Mark's prologue (1:1-8) as our text. Find a comfortable, quiet place to sit, then read the text slowly, carefully, and deliberately, either silently or aloud. Pay close attention to your breathing and your heart rate. After you've finished reading, sit silently in meditation on a word or a few words that stand out to you in the text.

A few examples:

How is the good news beginning?

Who is the good news?

After a period of several moments, read the text again—slowly, carefully, and deliberately. After you've finished reading, enter again into meditation, this time opening yourself up to what the text might be speaking to you and your life.

A few examples:

What is the good news that my soul most longs for?

What must be born within me so that I can hear God's voice more clearly?

After a period of several moments, read the text a third time, remembering your pacing. Then, return to meditation. This time, consider journaling (or speaking if in a small group) about what is being revealed to us by the words and their meaning, and by the larger story.

Then, read the text a fourth and final time, always aware of pacing. Afterward, return to meditation—this time, with a prayer. The Book of Common Prayer contains four Advent collects that are especially appropriate.

Here's a favorite:

Stir up your power, O Lord, and with great might come among us; and, because we are sorely hindered by our sins, let your bountiful grace and mercy speedily help and deliver us; through Jesus Christ our Lord, to whom, with you and the Holy Spirit, be honor and glory, now and for ever. Amen.

PRACTICE

Using the practice of *Lectio Divina*, spend time with this passage from Mark. To prepare your mind and heart, start with a moment of silence. Then read the passage slowly, perhaps two or three times. Think about a word or phrase that captures your attention. Then meditate on that word, asking why it resonates in this moment. Respond to God in prayer, and then rest in silence, savoring the word and contemplating what God is saying to you. Finally, consider how this word or phrase is calling you to act.

> Mark 1:1-8: *The beginning of the good news of Jesus Christ, the Son of God. As it is written in the prophet Isaiah: See, I am sending my messenger ahead of you, who will prepare your way; the voice of one crying out in the wilderness: "Prepare the way of the Lord, make*

his paths straight," John the baptizer appeared in the wilderness, proclaiming a baptism of repentance for the forgiveness of sins. And people from the whole Judean countryside and all the people of Jerusalem were going out to him, and were baptized by him in the river Jordan, confessing their sins. Now John was clothed with camel's hair, with a leather belt around his waist, and he ate locusts and wild honey. He proclaimed, "The one who is more powerful than I is coming after me; I am not worthy to stoop down and untie the thong of his sandals. I have baptized you with water; but he will baptize you with the Holy Spirit."

WEDNESDAY

Jesus enters the scene and is baptized in Mark 1:9 with no pomp or pageantry whatsoever. After all, John has told us that one more powerful than him was coming who would baptize with the Holy Spirit.

John's baptism of Jesus for the repentance of sins might cause us to ask: whose sins? The answer is given in verses 10 and 11:

> *And just as he was coming up out of the water, he saw the heavens torn apart and the Spirit descending like a dove on him. And a voice came from heaven, 'You are my Son, the Beloved; with you I am well pleased.'*

The phrase "Heavens torn apart..." is *schizomenous* in Greek, which means a violent splitting open. We hear similar words later in Mark 15:37-38: "Then Jesus gave a loud cry and breathed his last. And the curtain of the temple was torn in two, from top to bottom."

John baptizes Jesus for the repentance of sins and points us immediately to the answer to our question: our sins. In this Jesus whom John told us about, we find the gate to heaven torn open; we hear God's voice; we see the Spirit descending; our sins are forgiven. Sometimes the message we most need to receive comes from people in places and in ways that we can scarcely imagine.

Although we might not often hear them in this way, our own Baptismal Covenant contains radical attestations of both belief and practice. Because we believe in the God we meet in Jesus Christ by the power of the Holy Spirit, we proclaim our promise to respect the dignity of every human being, seek and serve Christ in all persons, and love our neighbor as ourselves—among other things. There are no asterisks or footnotes in the Baptismal Covenant, no wiggling out on a technicality or an exception. "All" means all; "every" means every; "love" means love. These are radical promises!

REFLECT

Advent offers us the space to hear even familiar stories in new ways. How might we hear and live into our Baptismal Covenant in new and deeper ways?

THURSDAY

In chapter four of Mark's Gospel, Jesus teaches about the kingdom of God. He uses the analogy of a farmer sowing seed in different types of soil, the imagery of a lamp hidden under a bushel basket, and the concept of a mustard seed. He also uses a second seed-like simile in verses 26-29, and unlike the others, this story is unique to Mark's Gospel. This time, someone has scattered seed on the ground, goes to bed, and is surprised and perplexed to find that the seed had grown overnight. I love this story, both for its simplicity and for what it reveals about how the kingdom of God works.

Many Christians conceive of nature as a closed system: nature runs all on its own, and God occasionally acts from outside nature, causing something supernatural (read: beyond what is natural) to happen. Scripture, however, reveals a markedly different truth about the relationship between God and nature.

God is not outside of nature in a removed, distant way; rather, God is, at every moment, holding the universe and all living things within it, in existence. It is God from whom all life is given, exists, and ends. If God were to hold God's breath, even for a second, all life in the universe would cease to exist. We are, at every moment, being suffused and animated by life-giving Spirit.

With this view of nature in mind, the parable of the seed that grows in the night reminds us that at every moment, God is active in our lives and in the world around us. Even in quiet, dark places, God is silently working to draw us into a deeper relationship with God. As we prepare for the coming of Christ in this Advent season, may we grow in our awareness of God's working in our midst at every moment, holding us tenderly in life and love, and drawing us toward the One we meet in the stable.

STUDY

Read Mark 4:26-29:

> *He also said, "The kingdom of God is as if someone would scatter seed on the ground, and would sleep and rise night and day, and the seed would sprout and grow, he does not know how. The earth produces of itself, first the stalk, then the head, then the full grain in the head. But when the grain is ripe, at once he goes in with his sickle, because the harvest has come."*

Where in your life have you experienced God quietly at work, even if you didn't understand that at the time? Are there areas in your life where you feel impatient for results? How can you trust the hidden growth there?

The seed grows while the farmer sleeps. What does this say to you about the need for control? During the season of Advent and beyond, how can you be more aware of God's presence in quiet and perhaps unseen ways?

FRIDAY

We cannot make it past the second verse of Mark's Gospel without encountering the word "prepare." Mark's opening scene picks up on Isaiah's prophetic pronouncement and reads as though we have arrived late to a drama already underway. We have work to do to catch up! But what is that work, exactly?

The culture around us has been stocking the shelves with wrapping paper and gifts since well before Thanksgiving. The Hallmark-ification of the holidays inverts the Christmas season, as though it ends rather than begins on December 25, and, in so doing, overlooks the season of Advent entirely. We can spin our wheels trying to resist this trend or, with Mark as our guide, we can choose a different way.

Notice where Mark's Gospel begins: away from Jerusalem, outside the city. This is intentional: to prepare for God to come among us and do a new thing in the person of Jesus, we have to get away from the noise and distractions of the world around us, and even those within us that claim our attention. Yes, noise and distraction are clearly visible on every store shelf and on every channel. But we cannot believe the lie that consumption is the gateway to happiness. God's grace is marvelously counter-cultural: it comes as a gift that we cannot buy because it is both priceless and absolutely free. It is not ours by earning or deserving but only and always through God's love.

Consider a few practical tips to help you stay grounded and focused during this holy season. Does that phone call really have to be taken during dinner time? Will the world come to an end if an email goes unanswered until tomorrow morning? Will the earth's axis spin in the opposite direction if we unplug ourselves from the 24-hour news cycle? Would a social media sabbatical be a gift we didn't know we needed in this season? Attend to the things in your life—both external and internal—that try to prevent you from stepping into the wilderness wonder of God.

Imagine for a moment what Mark might say to us this Advent, here in the twenty-first century. He would use no more words than absolutely necessary, his message would be direct and concise, and his focus would be laser-sharp: "Jesus Christ, the Son of God, is coming into the world!" Let us journey into the wilderness and prepare to receive him there with joy and gladness!

CONSIDER

What does "preparing" look like in your life beyond the usual holiday routines?

The Gospel of Mark begins in the wilderness, not the city. What does your "wilderness" look like?

Think about some of the suggestions in the reflection. Which could you choose to help you stay grounded and focused?

SATURDAY

As a priest, part of my vocation is to "minister the Word of God and the sacraments of the New Covenant, that the reconciling love of Christ may be known and received" (The Book of Common Prayer, p. 532). It is a hard and holy task, to be sure. The work of reconciliation is at the center of priestly ministry; in all that we do, both as Christians in general and clergy in particular, we are called to draw the circle wider so that God's reconciling love can spread, heal, and transform the world.

Shortly before I was ordained, a wise bishop told me that if I was going to be in the business of pronouncing forgiveness and working for reconciliation, then I also needed to be in the habit of asking for forgiveness and working for reconciliation in my own life. I took his advice and made an appointment with a priest to receive the sacrament of reconciliation.

I suspect my own experience is not unique: it is not an easy thing to confess the things you are least proud of to another human being! The sense of vulnerability and risk is palpable! What I came to learn, however, is that risk and vulnerability are the point, because it is only when we are willing to take that risk and open our hearts to that vulnerability that we receive God's grace.

The sacrament of reconciliation is available to anyone, and Advent is a particularly meaningful season for it. However, the grace of reconciliation is not restricted to the sacrament. Every person has relationships that have become strained by sin and stress, where God's grace can help us lean toward one another, rather than away from one another, or help us stand in our own integrity and name our needs and desires.

ACT

How might you engage in reconciliation in your own life? How might you ask for it, and how might you offer it? Consider writing a letter of reconciliation or forgiveness to someone as a starting place. You might also read through the rite of reconciliation, starting on page 446 of the Book of Common Prayer. Consider taking the vulnerable step and schedule a time with your priest for the sacrament of reconciliation.

LUKE

The Joy of the Incarnation

This Week's Writer

JERUSALEM JACKSON GREER

SUNDAY

The author of the Gospel of Luke is, despite the name, anonymous, as are the authors of all the gospels. However, tradition has assigned the Book of Acts, and this gospel—the longest, and, in my opinion, the most fulsome and beautiful of the accounts—to Luke, "the dearly loved physician" (Colossians 4:14, Common English Bible).

The themes of Luke easily lend themselves to the season of Advent:

> *Worship and Prayer: Jesus prays more in this gospel than any other*

> *Food and Meals: of the 19 meals mentioned in Luke, 13 are unique to his accounts*

Care of the Marginalized: Luke explicitly shows that the state of the poor and the outcast are the direct result of injustices.

Luke also elevates the ministry and role of women and uses a variety of images and titles for Jesus from both Jewish and Gentile traditions to create pathways of understanding for a wide range of contexts.

But my favorite theme of Luke is Present Salvation, which is a fancy way of saying that Jesus was born a savior. The salvation that Jesus offers didn't begin with his death and resurrection; it has always been an offering that he, God incarnate, has provided from his conception onward. Through Luke's lens, we come to understand that Jesus, from the beginning, offered salvation to all of humanity by giving us the gift of freedom from whatever stands between us and the flourishing whole life that God is always offering.

Luke shows us that what Jesus was and is most interested in is saving us from the things that break our relationships with God, with ourselves, and with each other, things like fear, greed, unbelief, selfishness, resentment, bigotry, unforgiveness, and violence.

As we travel this third week of Advent toward the birth of the Christ child, may we stop and remember that salvation is not something far off. It is not something we have to wait for or set aside for "someday." Salvation is here and now; it is ever-present. It is a gift that is meant to help heal and restore today. It is a salvation meant to free us from all the thoughts, postures, and habits that tear us apart, inside and out.

A few years ago, living in a little southern town, I would often pass yard signs that said "Jesus Saves" in bold script, with the name of the church in smaller print below. Occasionally, frustrated with the implication that all Jesus and Christianity are good for is a ticket to a sparkly afterlife, I would yell (inside my car) "from what? Jesus saves us from what?" as I drove past.

What I desperately wanted those signs to say was:

> *"Jesus saves me from shunning my LGBTQ neighbor."*
>
> *"Jesus saves me from thinking the immigrant deserves less than me."*
>
> *"Jesus saves me from ignoring how I benefit from the legacy of white supremacy in our systems."*
>
> *"Jesus saves me from harming myself."*
>
> *"Jesus saves me from accepting abuse as normal."*
>
> *"Jesus saves me from despair."*
>
> *"Jesus saves me from loneliness."*

"Jesus saves me from thinking there is no meaning in the world."

This third Week of Advent, I wonder if we could take some time to begin to name all the ways Jesus is saving us now, today. As we awaken to the realization that the joy of the incarnation is not something long ago or far ahead but rather here and now, can we, like Luke, invite others to see and name their salvation as well?

Stir up your power, O Lord, and with great might come among us; and, because we are sorely hindered by our sins, let your bountiful grace and mercy speedily help and deliver us; through Jesus Christ our Lord, to whom, with you and the Holy Spirit, be honor and glory, now and for ever. Amen.

MONDAY

I found out that I was pregnant with my youngest child when my best friend called to tell me she was pregnant with her first. "Guess what?" she crowed. "I'm pregnant!" came her squeal through my phone.

As she continued to chatter excitedly, I began doing the math. It didn't take long for me to realize that I, too, had missed some important days. One trip to the pharmacy later, I was suddenly making my own squealing phone call.

Her pregnancy was planned, and mine was a surprise, but both of us were happy and excited—not just to be expecting, but to be expecting together. To have someone else to travel with along the wonderful, nerve-wracking, often painful path of poking and prodding, growing and changing, preparing and waiting, that would lead us to spilling water and blood from our bodies as we ushered in new life, was a rare gift.

In Luke's Gospel, the relationship between Mary and Elizabeth is placed front and center. Their stories—their pregnancies and the events they entail—begin this account of the life of Jesus. These women who say "yes!" to their extraordinary circumstances are the first to deliver the Good News of God in Christ. They are the first to answer the call of the unexpected and the first to deliver the news that Love has come as flesh and blood to move into the neighborhood. And they are the first to put their literal lives on the line for the sake of the greatest love we will ever know.

Childbirth in the time of Mary and Elizabeth (and unfortunately still today for women at the margins of access to quality healthcare and support) was precarious at best. The dual weights of joy and fear would have been great for both of them. To carry these flesh-and-blood babies, sent from God as messengers and conduits of healing love, must have felt incredible. I mean, how remarkable to be so favored! And yet. They must also have known that carrying and delivering these holy world-changing babies might also mean their own deaths. No wonder Mary ran to Elizabeth. No wonder they sought each other's company and comfort.

Advent is a strange season. We hold the tension of waiting and celebrating. It is a season often filled with both hope and caution. With both dreams and disappointments. We want the world to be different; we are afraid to hope it can be.

By this point in the season, many of us have put up our Christmas trees, hung some stockings, attended some holiday parties, watched a holiday classic, baked some cookies, or at the very least hummed a carol or two as we wrapped our gifts. And yet, it is not Christmas yet. The gifts, pageants, candlelit worship services, and final revelry are still to come. Our remembering of Christ's birth is still to come; it is not yet here. We still have to wait and see.

Between the first Sunday of Advent and Christmas Eve, the potential for unexpected news, busted plans, and disappointment is vast and nerve-wracking. So many things could go wrong, and frankly, sometimes they do. There is a thinness to this season, a tenderness that asks us to say yes to entering into the mystery of God's love despite all the unknowns ahead. It asks us, like Elizabeth and Mary, to say yes with our lives, not just our words, to bring God's kingdom on earth, as it is in heaven.

REFLECT

Think of a time when you had unexpected news: a pregnancy, a job change, a diagnosis, a new relationship. Who did you share it with?

Elizabeth and Mary model not only their willingness to say yes to God but also the importance of relationship. In this period of waiting and watching, think about your relationships with others. Do some need nurturing? Could you send a word of gratitude to others? How do your relationships help you grow in faith and in a willingness to say yes to God?

TUESDAY

The Benedictine monastic tradition is steeped in the practice of *Lectio Divina*. But the roots of this practice can be traced back to the Apostle Paul's words: "The word is near you, on your lips and in your heart" (Romans 10:8-10).

Today, let's practice *Lectio Divina* with the "Song of Mary," which we most commonly call the *Magnificat*, found in Luke 1:46-55.

When I read over the *Magnificat* today, the phrase that stood out was "My soul." We are in Advent, which means that Christmas music is the soundtrack of the season wherever we go: stores, the car, holiday parties, Lessons & Carol services at church. The hymn "O Holy Night" is one of my favorites, especially as recorded by Sara Groves. Reflecting on Mary's words, these lines from the hymn rise to the surface: "Long lay the world in sin and error pining, Till he appeared, and the soul felt its worth." In these phrases, I hear the call to remember my soul, not just my intellect or my mind, but my soul, that thing deeper within, that goes beyond facts and feelings, to true knowing. Mary doesn't begin with "My mind proclaims the greatness of the Lord." She doesn't even begin with "My actions proclaim..." She begins with her soul: that unquantifiable essence that is her, made in the image of God.

All too often, I have been tempted to see the coming Jesus as the thing that illuminates our sin and greed, as if the world didn't realize how dirty it was until Jesus comes to walk among us and give his life for us. And yet, according to the songwriter and Luke, we, the humans on this earth, don't need help accessing feelings of shame or thoughts of worthlessness. We, and our weary souls, don't need help identifying our flaws and the ways we hurt ourselves and each other. What we do need is salvation: a salvation that reminds us that we, who are made in the image of God, are completely loved, and through this love, we—our weary souls and all—are worthy to proclaim the goodness of God in Christ with all authority, with all joy.

What if this Christmas we realized that Jesus does not come to reveal our brokenness but rather to reveal our belovedness? Jesus comes to reveal that even the people at the bottom of the social strata are worthy, not because of their intellect or success, but because they are a beloved children of God. It is from this knowledge that Mary can boldly sing her song. It is from this knowledge that I, too, can boldly proclaim the Good News.

PRACTICE

Using the practice of *Lectio Divina*, spend time with this passage.

Luke 1:46-55: And Mary said, "My soul magnifies the Lord, and my spirit rejoices in God my Savior, for he has looked with favor on the lowliness of his servant. Surely, from now on all generations will call me blessed; for the Mighty One has done great things for me, and holy is his name. His mercy is for those who fear him from generation to generation. He has shown strength with his arm; he has scattered the proud in the thoughts of their hearts. He has brought down the powerful from their thrones, and lifted up the lowly; he has filled the hungry with good things, and sent the rich away empty. He has helped his servant Israel, in remembrance of his mercy, according to the promise he made to our ancestors, to Abraham and to his descendants forever."

WEDNESDAY

A few years ago, while preparing for yet another Christmas pageant, I began to wonder: What would it be like to hear the story for the first time? What would it be like to watch or listen to this story being told without a lifetime of understanding where the story was headed? If I hadn't heard this story before, what would I notice?

So, I found a recording of the story, and I tried to listen, really listen, as if I were a stranger to the tale. And here is what I noticed as I researched: Advent and ultimately Christmas begin with a whole series of interruptions. Like a trail of breadcrumbs, we can follow the busted plans of a motley crew of ordinary people straight to the birth and life of Jesus. To begin, there's Joseph, a carpenter and betrothed fiancé of Mary, a young unwed mother-to-be. There's an innkeeper with a full house and shepherds out doing their job on an ordinary day. Later, some Magi notice something odd in the stars, and a misguided king named Herod seeks unchecked power. All these people—all of these characters in the story we all know so well—had their plans completely disrupted, delayed, postponed, or wiped out by a baby. By Jesus. By what we now call Christmas.

A lot of us put a lot of hope and effort into having a perfect Christmas. Adults, parents, grandparents, even children. When my dad was nine years old, he wrote a multi-page document on how to have "the best Christmas ever." This guide, mostly centered on how he would get past his pet dog to the tree on Christmas morning without waking everyone, included multiple contingency plans and step-by-step instructions on which toys to play with first, depending on the outcome. Unfortunately, his plans for a perfectly planned Christmas ended with the births of his four rowdy children!

Despite what social media and the movies tell us, Christmas was never—and never will be—about perfect parties or gifts, decorations or traditions. Instead, the only "perfect" we can rightly associate with Christmas is the perfect love of Christ, which drives out all fear. The only plan worth holding onto is the one that involves Holy Love becoming incarnate. And fair warning: this incarnation turns out to be a messy and complicated reality, because from the beginning until now, the very essence of Christmas has been rooted in ordinary humans saying yes to God even when it destroys our expectations, ruins our comfort, and defies convention.

I suppose that Mary, Joseph, the innkeeper, the shepherds, and the Magi could have said no to participating in the Greatest Story Ever Told. They could have told God to go sit on a log. They could have opted for safe and expected and well planned-out lives. They could have stayed home, stayed in the fields, not offered the barn. They could have rejected the invitation to follow God's call and turned away from all that was possible.

But they didn't say no. Thank God! They said yes. And then they went. One step in front of the other, no matter how bizarre the request or message from God. This is the invitation to all of us every Advent. To say yes again and again to allowing God to come into our lives, disrupting our agendas for the sake of transforming love.

REFLECT

For many of us, the second chapter of the Gospel of Luke offers the birth narrative that we most associate with Christmas: "In those days, a decree went out... " You might be able to shut your eyes and remember a wobbly retelling with children dressed in bed sheets and lopsided shawls over their heads. Taking a prompt from this reflection, try listening to or reading the narrative as if it was the first time. What do you see? Hear? Taste? Smell? What message most stands out to you in this experience?

THURSDAY

Once, as a priest was teaching me how to light and extinguish the altar candles, she mentioned that we never light the candle representing Christ first or extinguish it last. When I asked why, she simply shrugged and said, "Well, Jesus is always in community." That moment was a revelation.

From the relationship of the Trinity to Jesus's birth into a family, from his ministry with the twelve disciples to his dying on the cross between two criminals to his ascension into heaven to sit at the right of God (witnessed by the disciples), Jesus is rarely alone. And in the few examples we have of him on his own, he is seeking or returning to community.

That is one of the reasons why I love the story of Jesus calling his disciples in Luke 5.

This account begins with Jesus in a pickle. He has begun his ministry, apparently on his own, and he is gaining such popularity and having such an impact that the crowds following him are pressing in on him. He is overwhelmed, seemingly being forced from the beach into the sea. Looking to create some space between himself and the crowd, Jesus quickly retreats onto a boat, which turns out to be manned by Simon Peter.

By the time the story ends, Simon Peter, James, and John have all decided to leave the boats to follow Jesus. They have now become the first disciples, and Jesus is no longer a loner. He is once again part of a community.

A thorough reading of the New Testament will show all the ways in which Simon Peter needed Jesus, but, reading this story through the lens of Advent, what stands out to me is that Jesus also needed Simon Peter. He needed James and John. He, Jesus, light of the world, also needed community, just like us.

Why? Because, partially, as a human, Jesus was built for connection. The need to be in community is a basic human need that we each carry within us. And secondly, the work Jesus was sent to do, and later would call Simon Peter to do, and has since called us to do, is not a loner's work. It is communal work.

Loving our neighbors, feeding the hungry, taking care of the widows, welcoming the stranger, loving our enemies, raising the orphan, sheltering the unloved. None of this is work we can or should do on our own. It is weighty, holy, and taxing work, physically, emotionally, spiritually. It is not work anyone should carry on their shoulders alone.

This story reminds me that being in community is central to who Jesus is and who Jesus calls us to be. In Christmas , we remember that God is with us, by choice. God is in community with us because community is the way of love, the way of God.

STUDY

Read Luke 5:1-10:

> *Once while Jesus was standing beside the lake of Gennesaret, and the crowd was pressing in on him to hear the word of God, he saw two boats there at the shore of the lake; the fishermen had gone out of them and were washing their nets. He got into one of the boats, the one belonging to Simon, and asked him to put out a little way from the shore. Then he sat down and taught the crowds from the boat. When he had finished speaking, he said to Simon, "Put out into the deep water and let down your nets for a catch." Simon*

answered, "Master, we have worked all night long but have caught nothing. Yet if you say so, I will let down the nets." When they had done this, they caught so many fish that their nets were beginning to break. So they signaled their partners in the other boat to come and help them. And they came and filled both boats, so that they began to sink. But when Simon Peter saw it, he fell down at Jesus' knees, saying, "Go away from me, Lord, for I am a sinful man!" For he and all who were with him were amazed at the catch of fish that they had taken; and so also were James and John, sons of Zebedee, who were partners with Simon. Then Jesus said to Simon, "Do not be afraid; from now on you will be catching people." When they had brought their boats to shore, they left everything and followed him.

Have you ever thought about Jesus needing his disciples? What does this perspective tell you about the importance of community and connection? In your spiritual life, does community have a high priority? How can you be deliberate about creating and strengthening faithful connections?

FRIDAY

For several years, our family lived on a small farm in Central Arkansas. During that season, while the kids were still living at home, we accumulated a motley crew of farm critters: goats, hens and roosters, dogs (inside and outside ones), barn cats, and even a pet pig named Winston.

Each Advent, as we drew close to Christmas Eve, we worked as a family to clean the pens and coops in preparation for the Christ Child's arrival in the manger. Together we mucked out all the old straw and wood shavings, replacing them with fresh, fluffy bedding. We repaired broken nest boxes or feeders, patched holes, and mended fences. Finally, we made wreaths from evergreens we foraged from our wooded property line, embellishing them with garlands of popcorn and cranberries as treats for the birds. Our final act was to hang the wreaths on each animal habitat's door or gate, adding a bit of festooning to their rustic shelters.

This tradition is one of my most beloved memories from those years. There was something simple and holy in working together to prepare the mangers of our barnyard menagerie before we took the time to get ourselves ready for the big night.

At the beginning of this week, we celebrated Gaudete Sunday, the third Sunday of Advent. But before we reach *Gaudete* (which means "rejoice" in Latin), we are in the muck and mud of repentance. We are looking at all those things we have done and left undone in our relationships with God, each other, the earth, and even with ourselves. This is why we spend the first few weeks of Advent examining and hopefully repenting of these intentional and unintentional wrongs. We do this so that we can take the time needed to let them go, to add them to the compost pile of our lives, where all the old and rotten bits go to decompose until they are useful again, redeemed through the love of Christ.

As we move through the final days before the birth of Christ, it is time to throw the last of the muck out, rejoicing as we turn together from the clearing out to the adding in. We begin working together in joyful anticipation of the birth of Christ. We prepare with songs of glad tidings and prayers of thanksgiving, laying the foundation for a life built on grace and forgiveness. We gather our renewed obedience and faithfulness like evergreens and lash them into a wreath of Good News, stringing love for our neighbor and care for the poor into a garland with berries and popcorn as an adornment. Finally, we bring it all together, opening our hearts, our lives, and our community to all the ways that the love of Christ will enter in and change our world, again.

CONSIDER

What is the muck and mud in your life that needs cleaning?

What needs to be cleared out so that Christ can enter in?

SATURDAY

Last January, I received this text from a friend: "Is there still an abundance of eggs at camp? It's been a bad week. I now have many more families sheltering in place. Kids unable to go to school and staff delivering food, laundry detergent, etc. If there is an abundance, I could use more. One of our fathers was taken from the McDonald's drive-thru line down the street after he dropped off his daughter at school. He stopped for a cup of coffee that cost him his freedom."

Here at the camp, retreat center, and farm, where my husband and I are the co-executive directors, we raise layer hens. Thanks to the heat lamps in their coop, our gals are great layers even in the winter months, and since things are slower in both our kitchen and market during this time of year, we often have an excess, even after our team gets what they need.

So, it was easy to reply with a hearty, "Yes! We have plenty! I will let our farm manager know that all our excess comes to you until further notice."

I hate that this is necessary. I am grateful that we have something to offer.

A few years ago, after one of our children let us know they were transgender, I immediately texted my friend Chris, who is also a mother to a trans young adult. She knew all the questions I needed to be asked; she held space for all my thoughts, feelings, and wonderings—the ones that just needed a soft place to land as I processed all I was learning about my amazing offspring. She listened without judgment and advised when asked.

I did not expect this change in my child's identity. I am grateful I had a friend who was further ahead than me and could hold my hand as I changed course.

Once, during a particularly hard season when it seemed everything in my life was falling apart, my friend Jo sent me a box filled with yellow everything. Notebooks, candy, hair ties, a mug, and more. I think there was even a yellow gnome included!

I still carry some scars from that season. I also carry the warmth of that box deep in my bones.

Years ago, after a particularly violent moment in our country's history, my friend Marcus tweeted, "When the macro is overwhelming, switch to the micro." I have clung to this advice repeatedly during the turbulence of the past decade.

An excess of eggs, a long text exchange, a box of yellow trinkets. All of these things are quite micro. But each of them is imprinted on my heart. They have changed how I think about sharing resources, how I parent, and how I show up for others in their dark seasons. They won't change legislation or the hearts of thousands on their own. They won't be written about in history books. They are each as small as an empty feeding trough behind a full inn.

ACT

What micro acts have helped you through challenging times? Write a list and hold it near. Then, think about some small acts that you can offer to others—this day, this week, this season, this year.

JOHN

The Word Made Flesh

This Week's Writer

DEON K. JOHNSON

SUNDAY

Before shepherds or angels, before a manger or a census, John takes us back to the beginning of all things, to God's own life and desire. John's Gospel opens not with a birth story but with a confession of faith: "In the beginning was the Word." John is not interested in explaining how Jesus was born; he is intent on revealing why God chose to come among us at all.

Tradition remembers John as the beloved disciple, one who leaned close enough to Jesus to hear his heartbeat and lived long enough to ponder what love becoming flesh meant. John's Gospel reads less like a biography and more like a theological meditation shaped by memory, prayer, and wonder. John writes so that we might believe, not simply assent to ideas, but entrust our lives to the One who comes as light in the darkness.

Certain themes weave through this gospel like a steady refrain: light and life, belief and belonging, love and abiding. John speaks in symbols and contrasts, not to confuse us, but to draw us deeper, to beckon us further. Beyond the trappings and the outward appearances. Beyond the superficial and the sundry into the deep mystery. He invites us to linger, to listen, to look beyond the surface. This is a gospel that insists God is not distant or abstract but intimately involved in the life of the world.

At the heart of it all is the astonishing and awesome claim of the Incarnation: "And the Word became flesh and lived among us." Not appeared to us. Not hovered above us. Not removed from us. Lived among us. The eternal Word through whom all things were made takes on flesh, our flesh, with all its fragility and limitation. This is not a sentimental story. It is a radical act of love. The enfleshment of God declares that there is no place God will not go, no experience God will not enter, to draw us closer in love.

The mystery of the Incarnation is not only that the Word became flesh once, in first-century Palestine. It is that the Word continues to take flesh, again and again, in our lives and in our world. Whenever grace breaks through fear, whenever truth is spoken in love, whenever compassion takes root in places of pain, God is once more dwelling among us.

John reminds us that the Word becoming flesh is not primarily about our longing for God, but about God's yearning for us. God does not wait for us to get it right or make ourselves worthy. God comes near. God abides. God chooses relationship over distance, vulnerability over power.

We often cling to the familiar trappings of the Incarnation: the manger, the angels, the shepherds. And those stories matter. But John gently strips them away so we can see what remains. Once the angels' song has faded, once the shepherds return to their fields, once the holy night gives way to ordinary days, we are left with this profound truth: God with us.

John's Gospel calls us to prepare to make room for God's glory revealed in unexpected places and uninvited people. It is to trust that the Word still takes flesh, still dwells among us, still draws us, patiently, persistently, passionately, toward the heart of God, full of grace and truth.

The challenge before us is not merely to celebrate the incarnation but to live it. To see Christ born again among us, in each new day, in every act of compassion, in each encounter with the other. The Word has become flesh. The divine has taken up residence in the ordinary. Joy to the world!

Purify our conscience, Almighty God, by your daily visitation, that your Son Jesus Christ, at his coming, may find in us a mansion prepared for himself; who lives and reigns with you, in the unity of the Holy Spirit, one God, now and for ever. Amen.

MONDAY

She was angry at God.

As she strode through the cemetery, having just buried her only brother, my grandmother gave God an earful. She had cared for him through his long illness until she couldn't physically do so. It broke her heart to admit him into a care community. Then he died less than two weeks after leaving her care.

She was angry at God. She used words that polite grandmothers never knew, much less said out loud, and to God, no less. And yet, that evening, she gathered her Bible and her prayer book and prayed Evening Prayer, just as she had every day before.

She was angry at God, and still, she remained on speaking terms.

I learned something essential about faith from my grandmother, long before I had phrases like Incarnation or the Word made flesh. As a child, I wasn't sure what to make of her actions that day. As an adult, I see it as one of the most honest acts of faith I have ever witnessed.

The Word made flesh means that we are not left alone at any time in our lives—not in joy and certainly not in grief. If God has taken on flesh, then there is no human emotion that is foreign to God. Anger, sorrow, confusion, longing—all of it has been entered into, held, and redeemed. My grandmother did not turn away from God in her pain; she turned toward God, trusting that God could bear her anguish. And God did.

To confess Jesus as fully divine and fully human is to trust that God knows our lives from the inside. Jesus does not hover above human experience; he lives it. He weeps at the grave of a friend. He knows hunger and exhaustion. He cries out in abandonment. He gets irritated and angry in the temple. He despairs of the city of Jerusalem. The Incarnation tells us that God is not offended by our honesty or threatened by our doubt. We can be angry, frustrated, or not even on speaking terms with God, and still, God remains with us.

The Word with us assures us that faith is not a solo act. We do not navigate the ups and downs of life on our own strength. God walks with us through valley lows and mountain highs, through moments of clarity and seasons of silence. Even when we feel distant from God, God is not distant from us. The Incarnation is God's promise to stay.

This understanding shapes my faith by grounding it not in perfection, but in possibility. Faith is not about having the right answers or even having it all together. It is about trust—trusting that God's love is steady even when our love wavers. Jesus's humanity gives us permission to be fully human with all our faults, failings, and falterings. Jesus's divinity gives us hope that love is stronger than death and that nothing in our lives is beyond God's redeeming presence.

The Word made flesh draws us into something larger than ourselves. Christ gathers all of creation into the life of God. We are invited into the unbroken and infinite circle of divine love that is the life of the Trinity, where grief and joy, anger and hope, humanity and holiness are held together. We do not journey in faith alone. We journey with a God who has chosen, forever, to be with us.

REFLECT

The grandmother's response is raw and real. She was angry with God, yet she didn't turn her back on God. Have you encountered situations in which you've held both anger and faith, grief and trust? Are there emotions you've been hesitant to bring to God, fearing they might be too much, too honest, or too unfaithful?

What would it look like to believe that God can hold your full story, not just the parts that feel polished or appropriate?

TUESDAY

Today, using the practice of *Lectio Divina*, let us start with the first words from John's Gospel.

"In the beginning was the Word." Before time. Before the noise. Before the need to prove ourselves. Before the fall. Before "before" was the Word. John takes us back, as if to remind us that before we did anything, before we earned anything, before we got it right or wrong, grace already was. The Word was with God. The Word was God. And this Word did not remain distant or abstract but became flesh and lived among us. Right in the middle of the messiness of the human family, grace upon grace took up residence.

"From his fullness we have all received, grace upon grace." Not some. Not a select few. All. Grace layered upon grace, gift stacked upon gift, mercy that does not run out. Grace is being able to stand up when the world tells us to sit down. Grace is speaking up when everything says to be silent. Grace upon grace is knowing that even in the valley of the shadow, God is with us.

And yet, receiving grace is hard. We live in a society that measures worth by productivity, by output, by merit. We are trained to believe that what we receive must be earned, that rest must be justified, that love must be deserved. In such a world, grace upon grace feels almost offensive. It refuses to play by the rules of Empire. It exposes systems built on scarcity, coercion, and control. Receiving grace is revolutionary because it says, "My life has value not because of what I produce, but because of who God is."

The Word becoming flesh means we can no longer settle for what the great twentieth-century theologian Deitrich Bonhoeffer called cheap grace, grace that asks nothing of us and changes nothing in us. Incarnate grace costs God everything and invites everything from us in return. If grace has any meaning, it must move through us, not stop with us. Pray for the courage to receive what we did not earn and to release what we have been freely given.

John's Gospel draws us back to the beginning, echoing God's blessing of the Sabbath—not simply good, but very good. Grace upon grace invites us to rest in God's fullness, to stop striving long enough to remember that we are already held. Sit with that fullness. Let it settle. Let it soften what has grown hard. Let it release that which has been held captive in your heart.

As you rise, may you have the courage not only to accept the grace you have been given, but to advance it, freely, generously, boldly, so that the world might glimpse, through us, the Word still becoming flesh.

PRACTICE

Using the practice of *Lectio Divina*, spend time with this passage from John.

> John 1:1-18: *In the beginning was the Word, and the Word was with God, and the Word was God. He was in the beginning with God. All things came into being through him, and without him not one thing came into being. What has come into being in him was life, and the life was the light of all people. The light shines in the darkness, and the darkness did not overcome it.*
>
> *There was a man sent from God, whose name was John. He came as a witness to testify to the light, so that all might believe through him. He himself was not the light, but he came to testify to the light. The*

true light, which enlightens everyone, was coming into the world.

He was in the world, and the world came into being through him; yet the world did not know him. He came to what was his own, and his own people did not accept him. But to all who received him, who believed in his name, he gave power to become children of God, who were born, not of blood or of the will of the flesh or of the will of man, but of God.

And the Word became flesh and lived among us, and we have seen his glory, the glory as of a father's only son, full of grace and truth. (John testified to him and cried out, "This was he of whom I said, 'He who comes after me ranks ahead of me because he was before me.'") From his fullness we have all received, grace upon grace. The law indeed was given through Moses; grace and truth came through Jesus Christ. No one has ever seen God. It is God the only Son, who is close to the Father's heart, who has made him known.

WEDNESDAY

The flame of the Paschal candle flickers, grounding the moment in eternity. Shards of sunlight spill across the congregation as young and old, believer and skeptic, gather shoulder to shoulder around the font. For a brief, holy instant, time loosens its grip. The air is thick with the scent of wax and chrism.

Water splashes. A child laughs. Her delighted giggle echoes through the space as her father lifts her from the font, both soaked in the waters of new birth. She reaches back, unwilling to leave the warmth, and the congregation responds with laughter that sounds a lot like joy.

"I baptize you..."

A rapturous Amen fills the room.

"You are sealed by the Holy Spirit and marked as Christ's own forever."

A lone voice begins a familiar hymn, and then another, until the room is carried by song. People step forward, touching the water, remembering their own sealing and marking, their own beginning.

Later, that same flame burns as mourners gather. Tears re-baptize grieving faces. Stories are told, prayers rise, and memory fills the space where absence now lives.

"I am the resurrection and I am the life..."

A mournful Amen fills the room.

"All of us go down to the dust. Yet even at the grave we make our song; Alleluia! Alleluia! Alleluia!"

Birth and farewell, laughter and loss, grief and glory, are held together by a single light and a single song, whispering that nothing offered to God is ever truly lost.

That simple Paschal light, burning from baptism to burial, reminds us of our own light shared and yet undimmed. The light of Christ is carried by those who sit with the grieving and do not rush the silence, by those who speak truth with courage and tenderness, by those who show up again and again when it would be easier to turn away. Parents and grandparents, teachers and mentors, friends and strangers, so many have helped bear Christ's light, often without knowing it. They have reflected God's presence simply by being fully present.

So it is with God's light in the world. It often comes through small openings, almost imperceptible cracks and chips in the armor of the world. The light seeps in through acts of kindness, moments of courage, lives offered in love. Christ's light does not overwhelm; it invites. It finds its way into places marked by death and speaks resurrection. It streams into the ordinary and the broken and declares that God is still at work.

Those who have borne Christ's light for me are like that flickering Paschal flame: not the source of the light, but faithful openings through which God's grace has shone and is shared. You are the light that calls others to the One Light through whom we have glimpsed the hope, healing, and holiness of God with us.

REFLECT

When have you experienced moments—like baptism or farewell—where time seemed to stand still and something sacred broke through? How do those moments shape your understanding of God's presence in both joy and grief? When you think about your own life, where do you see the "single light" holding together both beginnings and endings, laughter and loss?

THURSDAY

The sun stood high over Jacob's well, unforgiving, unrelenting, and unflinching, as if even the shadows had grown tired. Noonday is no time for gathering water, not if you can help it. And yet she came anyway, alone, eyes shaded, jar balanced, heart guarded. This was safer than the whispers, safer than the looks.

Then there was a man sitting by the well. A stranger. A Jew. A boundary already crossed.

"Give me a drink."

The request hangs in the air like a dare. He should not speak to her. She knows this. He knows this. And yet he does. The conversation moves like water over stone, slow, guarded at first, then deeper. Living water, he calls it. Water that quenches thirst forever. She laughs, half-skeptical, half-hopeful. Heatstroke maybe. Everyone promises relief. No one ever delivers.

"Go, call your husband."

The truth spills out before she can stop it. There have been many. And the one she lives with now is not her husband. She braces for judgment. It never comes.

Instead, Jesus sees her. All of her. The ache. The longing. The faith she has carried quietly, stubbornly. And then he says it plain and impossible and true: "I am he."

The jar is left behind. She runs back to the village, breathless, uncontained.

"Come and see a man who told me everything."

By the well, ordinary water has become holy. A woman once defined by shame becomes the prophet of good news. Thirst turns into testimony. And in that meeting, unexpected, inconvenient, grace-filled God shows once more that no one is invisible, and no life is beyond redemption.

While John 1 gives us the poetry and theology "the Word became flesh and lived among us," John 4 shows us what that looks like in lived, human reality. John insists that incarnation leads to transformation and witness. The woman leaves her water jar behind and becomes a bearer of good news to the very community that had rejected her. The Word who came to dwell among us now dwells within her witness. God's presence moves outward, taking flesh in her voice and courage.

If John 1 tells us that God became flesh, John 4 shows us why: so that no one is beyond the reach of living water, and no place is too ordinary or too broken for God to dwell.

STUDY

Read John 4:1-42:

> *Now when Jesus learned that the Pharisees had heard, "Jesus is making and baptizing more disciples than John" —although it was not Jesus himself but his disciples who baptized—he left Judea and started back to Galilee. But he had to go through Samaria. So he came to a Samaritan city called Sychar, near the plot of ground that Jacob had given to his son Joseph. Jacob's well was there, and Jesus, tired out by his journey, was sitting by the well. It was about noon.*
>
> *A Samaritan woman came to draw water, and Jesus said to her, "Give me a drink." (His disciples had gone to the city to buy food.) The Samaritan woman said to him, "How is it that you, a Jew, ask a drink of me,*

a woman of Samaria?" (Jews do not share things in common with Samaritans.) Jesus answered her, "If you knew the gift of God, and who it is that is saying to you, 'Give me a drink,' you would have asked him, and he would have given you living water." The woman said to him, "Sir, you have no bucket, and the well is deep. Where do you get that living water? Are you greater than our ancestor Jacob, who gave us the well, and with his sons and his flocks drank from it?" Jesus said to her, "Everyone who drinks of this water will be thirsty again, but those who drink of the water that I will give them will never be thirsty. The water that I will give will become in them a spring of water gushing up to eternal life." The woman said to him, "Sir, give me this water, so that I may never be thirsty or have to keep coming here to draw water."

Jesus said to her, "Go, call your husband, and come back." The woman answered him, "I have no husband." Jesus said to her, "You are right in saying, 'I have no husband'; for you have had five husbands, and the one you have now is not your husband. What you have said is true!" The woman said to him, "Sir, I see that you are a prophet. Our ancestors worshiped on this mountain, but you say that the place where people must worship is in Jerusalem." Jesus said to her, "Woman, believe me, the hour is coming when you will worship the Father neither on this mountain nor in Jerusalem.

You worship what you do not know; we worship what we know, for salvation is from the Jews. But the hour is coming, and is now here, when the true worshipers will worship the Father in spirit and truth, for the Father seeks such as these to worship him. God is spirit, and those who worship him must worship in spirit and truth." The woman said to him, "I know that Messiah is coming" (who is called Christ). "When he comes, he will proclaim all things to us." Jesus said to her, "I am he, the one who is speaking to you."

Just then his disciples came. They were astonished that he was speaking with a woman, but no one said, "What do you want?" or, "Why are you speaking with her?" Then the woman left her water jar and went back to the city. She said to the people, "Come and see a man who told me everything I have ever done! He cannot be the Messiah, can he?" They left the city and were on their way to him.

Meanwhile the disciples were urging him, "Rabbi, eat something." But he said to them, "I have food to eat that you do not know about." So the disciples said to one another, "Surely no one has brought him something to eat?" Jesus said to them, "My food is to do the will of him who sent me and to complete his work. Do you not say, 'Four months more, then comes the harvest'? But I tell you, look around you, and see how the fields are ripe for harvesting. The reaper is already receiving wages and is gathering fruit for eternal life, so that sower and reaper may rejoice together. For here the saying holds true, 'One sows and another reaps.' I sent you to reap that for which you did not labor. Others have labored, and you have entered into their labor."

Many Samaritans from that city believed in him because of the woman's testimony, "He told me everything I have ever done." So when the Samaritans came to him, they asked him to stay with them; and he stayed there two days. And many more believed because of his word. They said to the woman, "It is no longer because of what you said that we believe, for we have heard for ourselves, and we know that this is truly the Savior of the world."

This is the longest conversation Jesus has with anyone that is recorded in scripture. Why do you think this story is important for followers? What are some of the lessons that you take from the encounter?

At the end of the passage, it says, "Many Samaritans from that city believed in him because of the woman's testimony." When have you offered your testimony to others about Jesus? What holds you back from proclaiming the Good News?

FRIDAY

"From his fullness we have all received, grace upon grace." (John 1:16)

At the height of apartheid in South Africa, thousands of women and men were disappeared. Their lives snuffed out as if they hadn't existed. Mothers, sons, fathers, daughters, cousins, aunts, friends, lovers, left with the grief of the unknown. No final rites. No graves to visit. No parting words. Just disappeared lives. Taken in the dark of night by men in masks.

A widowed mother lost her only child. Despite her cries and her tears, they took him. Unmoved by the frantic pleas of a mother for her son. He was numbered among the disappeared.

After the fall of apartheid came truth and reconciliation. One of the men who stole into her house that faithful night came forward. As she stood there, he shared in detail the kidnapping, torture, and brutal murder of her son, hoping that the truth would set him free from the burden he had carried.

"You took my son from me!" They were waiting for the venom, for the call for vengeance. "I cooked for my son every Sunday. You took my son from me, and now you will take his place. Your children will become my grandchildren; your family will become my family." Grace upon grace.

Grace is the relentless generosity of God. It is not grace as a one-time gift or a limited supply, but grace layered upon grace given, received, and then given again. Grace meets us where we are, and then meets us again when we fall short, and again when we begin once more.

Grace upon grace means that God does not tire of us. It means that God's love is not exhausted by our mistakes, missteps, or misdeeds. We mess up. Sometimes we mess up mightily. We try again. And in that space between failure and beginning anew, grace is already waiting. Not as punishment withheld, but as love freely offered.

I experience grace upon grace most clearly in moments when I know I have not gotten it right, when words spoken too quickly cannot be taken back, when fear has shaped my choices more than faith, when I have failed to love as boldly as I am called to love. And yet, even then, I am not cast aside. There is room to repent, room to return, room to begin again. God's mercy does not shame; it restores.

Grace is not a ladder we climb toward God; it is the steady presence of God who comes down to us, again and again. Grace upon grace is the assurance that our lives are not defined by our worst moments, but by God's faithfulness. We mess up. We try again. And every time we do, we discover that we are met not with scarcity, but with an abundance of God's amazing grace.

CONSIDER

How does the story of the grieving mother shape your understanding of grace, especially in situations of deep injustice or suffering?

When have you experienced "grace upon grace," of being met with love and mercy when you least deserved or expected it?

What would it look like for you to extend grace to someone else? How can you extend grace not as a one-time act, but as an ongoing practice of generosity?

SATURDAY

Who sparked your faith? Who first made the Good News of Jesus come alive for you? We do not often pause to ask these questions, yet in Advent, a season shaped by waiting and expectation, returning to the beginnings of our faith feels especially fitting.

For me, it was my grandmother. She taught me how to pray, brought me to church, and made sure I knew God loved me long before I had language for theology or doctrine. Her Book of Common Prayer and her Bible were her most treasured possessions. Through her, I encountered a faith that was embodied and relational, woven into the rhythms of daily life.

Each morning, she prayed, and each evening she gave thanks, rain or shine, in joy and in sorrow. She never preached a sermon or wrote a theological reflection. She lived her faith. In her, I learned that following Jesus is not primarily about words, but about how we love, how we show up, and how we serve.

Worship, as I came to know it, was not about mastering doctrine but about belonging to a community that held us, corrected us, nourished us, and sent us back into the world to love and serve. Worship is both anchor and compass. It grounds us in who God is and reminds us of who we are becoming. In the noise and pressure of life, common prayer draws us back to what matters most: God with us.

Week by week, prayer shapes us in quiet ways. Confession tells the truth about us; absolution tells the truth about God. At the table, ordinary bread and wine become bearers of grace. We come not because we are worthy, but because we are hungry. The Word continues to take flesh in community and in us.

Faith is never solitary. We pray, sing, grieve, and rejoice together. And in this season of Advent, we remember that the Word who was in the beginning still chooses to dwell among us, full of grace and truth, lighting our darkness and inviting us, again and again, into life.

ACT

Who sparked your faith? Write about how that person modeled love and service. If they are still here, share the reflection with them.

Ask yourself: are you behaving in a way to be the spark for someone else? What changes can you make so you make the word of God come alive for others?

STUDY GUIDE
For Groups

There are many ways to use *Gospel Voices* as a foundation for group study. You might use the daily questions and prompts at the end of each devotion as a starting point for discussion. You could also employ the prayer practice of *Lectio Divina* with other excerpts from each gospel.

This guide reflects on some broad themes of how each gospel shares the birth story in unique ways. We encourage you to adapt this guide to best fit your context and participants.

Matthew

OPENING PRAYER

Almighty God, give us grace to cast away the works of darkness, and put on the armor of light, now in the time of this mortal life in which your Son Jesus Christ came to visit us in great humility; that in the last day, when he shall come again in his glorious majesty to judge both the living and the dead, we may rise to the life immortal; through him who lives and reigns with you and the Holy Spirit, one God, now and for ever. Amen.

READ & REFLECT

Read aloud the first two chapters of Matthew.

Your story matters: By starting with Jesus's genealogy, Matthew tells us that our stories matter and that God works through real lives and real people, not perfect ones. Consider some of the unexpected people in Jesus's lineage. Tamar disguised herself as a prostitute and seduced her father-in-law. Ruth was originally a Gentile, not a Jew, yet in her faithfulness, she marries into a Jewish family, converts, and becomes the great-grandmother of King David. One of Judah's most wicked leaders, King Manasseh, was a pagan who sacrificed his own son, yet he, too, is listed.

Take a few minutes to write down your genealogy and respond to these questions:

> *What are some characteristics of your ancestors that you're thankful for?*
>
> *What areas are messy?*
>
> *What does the inclusion of some of these unexpected people in the lineage tell you about Jesus?*

If you feel led, share a story or two about your family with the group.

PRACTICE

Explore a passage from the Gospel of Matthew using the ancient prayer practice of *Lectio Divina*. This practice has four parts: read (*lectio*), meditate or reflect (*meditatio*), pray or respond (*oratio*), and contemplate or rest (*contemplatio*).

Here are some suggestions:

> *Matthew 1:18–25 (Joseph's trust)*
>
> *Matthew 5:1-12 (The Beatitudes)*
>
> *Matthew 6:9-13 (The Lord's Prayer)*
>
> *Matthew 17:1-9 (The Transfiguration)*

CLOSING PRAYER

We thank you, heavenly Father, for the witness of your apostle and evangelist Matthew to the Gospel of your Son our Savior; and we pray that, after his example, we may with ready wills and hearts obey the calling of our Lord to follow him; through Jesus Christ our Lord, who lives and reigns with you and the Holy Spirit, one God, now and for ever. Amen.

Mark

OPENING PRAYER

Merciful God, who sent your messengers the prophets to preach repentance and prepare the way for our salvation: Give us grace to heed their warnings and forsake our sins, that we may greet with joy the coming of Jesus Christ our Redeemer; who lives and reigns with you and the Holy Spirit, one God, now and for ever. Amen.

READ & REFLECT

Read aloud the first chapter of Mark.

Wilderness as a starting place: Mark begins in the wilderness, in a place of discomfort, honesty, and transformation. Where is the "wilderness" in your life right now? What feels uncertain, quiet, or stripped down?

Take a few minutes to reflect and respond to these questions:

> *Where do you sense God calling you to step away from noise or distraction?*
>
> *What might God be preparing in you in this season?*

If you feel led, share a time when you experienced growth in a difficult or uncertain season.

PRACTICE

Explore a passage from the Gospel of Mark using the ancient prayer practice of *Lectio Divina*. This practice has four parts: read (*lectio*), meditate or reflect (*meditatio*), pray or respond (*oratio*), and contemplate or rest (*contemplatio*).

Here are some suggestions:

Mark 1:1–8 (The voice in the wilderness)

Mark 1:9–13 (The baptism of Jesus and temptation in the wilderness)

Mark 1:16–20 (The calling of the first disciples)

Mark 13:33-37 (Stay awake)

CLOSING PRAYER

Almighty God, by the hand of Mark the evangelist you have given to your Church the Gospel of Jesus Christ the Son of God: We thank you for this witness, and pray that we may be firmly grounded in its truth; through Jesus Christ our Lord, who lives and reigns with you and the Holy Spirit, one God, for ever and ever. Amen.

Luke

OPENING PRAYER

Stir up your power, O Lord, and with great might come among us; and, because we are sorely hindered by our sins,let your bountiful grace and mercy speedily help and deliver us; through Jesus Christ our Lord, to whom, with you and the Holy Spirit, be honor and glory, now and for ever. Amen.

READ & REFLECT

Read aloud the first two chapters of Luke.

Relationships matter: Luke begins with connection, with Mary and Elizabeth sharing stories and offering companionship as they wait. This waiting reflects the tension of Advent: hope and uncertainty, joy and fear. But Luke shows us that God is always with us, even in the midst of difficulty.

Take a few minutes to reflect:

> *Who has walked with you in seasons of waiting or uncertainty?*
>
> *How have your relationships shaped your faith?*
>
> *What do you think about the idea that faith unfolds in community, not in isolation?*

If you feel led, share a time when someone helped carry hope for you or a special relationship that strengthened your ability to trust God.

PRACTICE

Explore a passage from the Gospel of Luke using the ancient prayer practice of *Lectio Divina*. This practice has four parts: read (*lectio*), meditate or reflect (*meditatio*), pray or respond (*oratio*), and contemplate or rest (*contemplatio*).

Here are some suggestions:

Luke 1:26–38 (The Annunciation to Mary)

Luke 1:39–45 (Mary and Elizabeth)

Luke 1:46–55 (The Magnificat)

Luke 2:1–20 (The birth of Jesus)

CLOSING PRAYER

Almighty God, who inspired your servant Luke the physician to set forth in the Gospel the love and healing power of your Son: Graciously continue in your Church this love and power to heal, to the praise and glory of your Name; through Jesus Christ our Lord, who lives and reigns with you, in the unity of the Holy Spirit, one God, now and for ever. Amen.

John

OPENING PRAYER

Purify our conscience, Almighty God, by your daily visitation, that your Son Jesus Christ, at his coming, may find in us a mansion prepared for himself; who lives and reigns with you, in the unity of the Holy Spirit, one God, now and for ever. Amen.

READ & REFLECT

Read aloud the first chapter of John.

In the beginning: Unlike the other gospels, John begins with eternity, inviting us to see Jesus not only as a person in history, but as the very presence of God entering the world and coming close. God in Jesus is fully present in human life, with all its beauty and brokenness.

Take a few minutes to reflect:

> *What stands out to you about how John introduces Jesus?*
>
> *How does this "cosmic" beginning change your understanding of Advent?*
>
> *What does it mean to you that God chose to "live among us"?*

If you feel led, share where you see God "taking flesh" in the world today. What are some ways your life can become a place where others encounter God's presence?

PRACTICE

Explore a passage from the Gospel of John using the ancient prayer practice of *Lectio Divina*. This practice has four parts: read (*lectio*), meditate or reflect (*meditatio*), pray or respond (*oratio*), and contemplate or rest (*contemplatio*).

Here are some suggestions:

John 1:1–18 (The Word became flesh)

John 4:1–26 (Jesus and the Samaritan woman)

John 11:32–36 (Jesus weeps)

John 20:11–18 (Mary Magdalene at the tomb)

CLOSING PRAYER

Shed upon your Church, O Lord, the brightness of your light, that we, being illumined by the teaching of your apostle and evangelist John, may so walk in the light of your truth, that at length we may attain to the fullness of eternal life; through Jesus Christ our Lord, who lives and reigns with you and the Holy Spirit, one God, for ever and ever. Amen.

About the Authors

Tina Francis is a writer, photographer, and seminarian pursuing the priesthood in the Episcopal Church. Born to South Indian parents, raised in Dubai, shaped in Canada and Seattle, and now living in Austin, Texas, she carries many homes in her bones—an atlas of memory and migration.

Jerusalem Jackson Greer is co-executive director and agrarian minister for the Procter Center, an Episcopal farm, camp, and retreat center in London, Ohio, and the Episcopal Diocese of Southern Ohio. The former manager of evangelism and discipleship for the Episcopal Church under Presiding Bishop Michael Curry, she is an associate of the Community of Saint Mary, Southern Province, and a co-host of the *Spade, Spoon, Soul* podcast.

Deon K. Johnson is the first openly gay, first black, and first immigrant bishop to lead the Diocese of Missouri. Born and raised on the island of Barbados, he and his family now live in Webster Groves, Missouri. He enjoys cooking, photography, hiking, and being an armchair movie critic.

Marshall Jolly is the rector of St. Thaddeus Episcopal Church and president of Mead Hall Episcopal School in Aiken, South Carolina. He holds degrees in theology and other subjects from Transylvania University and Emory University and enjoys running, reading, and golf. He and his wife are looked after by Hambrick, a nine-pound Himalayan cat with a huge personality.

About Forward Movement

Forward Movement inspires disciples and empowers evangelists. As a discipleship ministry, we create and publish books, daily reflections, studies for small groups, and online resources. People around the world read daily devotions through *Forward Day by Day*, which is also available in Spanish (*Adelante Dia a Dia*) and Braille, online, as a podcast, and as an app for smartphones.

We actively seek partners across the church and look for ways to provide resources that inspire and challenge. A ministry of the Episcopal Church since 1935, Forward Movement is a nonprofit organization funded by sales of resources and gifts from generous donors.

To learn more about Forward Movement and our work, visit us at ForwardMovement.org or VenAdelante.org. We are delighted to be doing this work and invite your prayers and support.